W9-BLH-595
R03000 28506

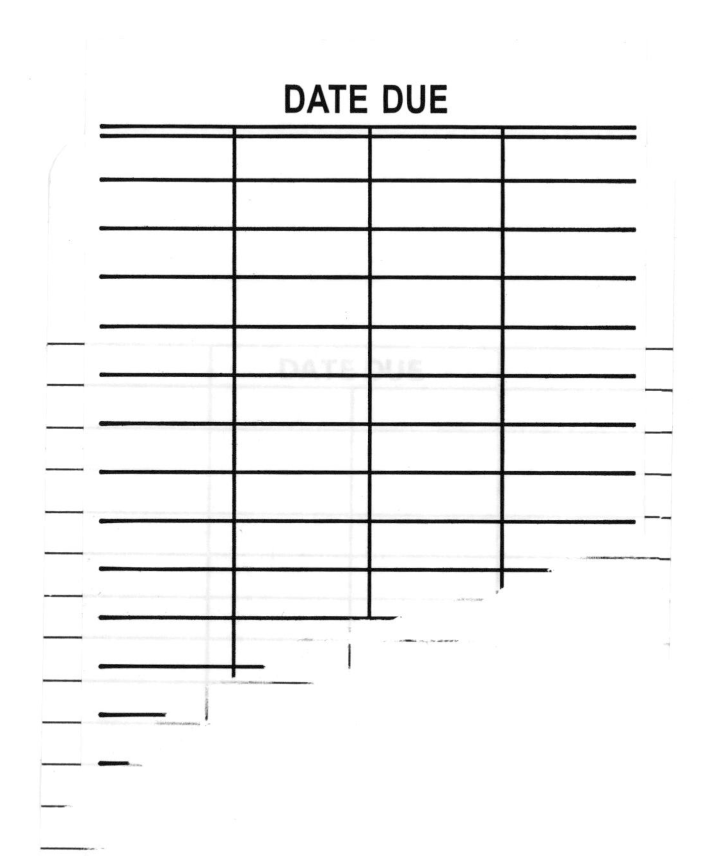
DATE DUE

Science Experiments

ROCKS AND MINERALS

by
John Farndon

BENCHMARK BOOKS
MARSHALL CAVENDISH
NEW YORK

Marshall Cavendish Corporation

99 White Plains Road

Tarrytown, New York 10591

Created by Brown Partworks Limited

Library of Congress Cataloging-in-Publication Data

Farndon, John.
Rocks and minerals / by John Farndon.
p. cm. – (Science experiments)
Includes index.
Summary: Discusses the physical properties of various rocks and minerals and gives instructions for experiments that identify their unique characteristics.
ISBN 0-7614-1468-1
1. Rocks–Experiments–Juvenile literature. 2. Minerals–Experiments–Juvenile literature. [1. Rocks–Experiments. 2. Minerals–Experiments. 3. Experiments.] I. Title. II. Series.
QE432.2 .F37 2003
549'.078–dc21

2002000908

Printed in Hong Kong

PHOTOGRAPHIC CREDITS

t – top; b – bottom; c – center; l – left; r – right

Bruce Coleman: p18 P Kaya
Corbis: p21 Jonathan Blair, p25 Galen Rowell
Heidelberg Cement: p15
NASA: p5
NHPA: p6 Kevin Schafer; p12 John Shaw; p16 Daniel Heuclin; p20 David Woodfall; p26 G I Bernard; p27 Dan Griggs
Science & Society Picture Library: p8 Science Museum
Turkish Information Office: p14
USDA NRCS: p4, p10 Tim McCabe

Step-by-step photography throughout: Martin Norris

Front Cover: Bruce Coleman: P Kaya

Contents

WHAT ARE ROCKS?

Rocks are the hard material that make up the earth's surface. Every mountain and hill, every valley and plain, every island and every continent in the world is made of rock. Even the ocean bed is made of rock.

All these features of the earth's surface are just the top of the earth's thin, rigid shell. This shell, or crust, is a layer of solid rock wrapped right round the earth and is between 4 and 56 miles (6–90 km) thick.

Rocks are not always visible on the surface, although they can be seen in quarries and cliffs. They are usually underneath vegetation, soil, or roads and buildings. Yet they are always there, just a little way below the surface.

In mountains, the rocks that make up the earth's surface are visible as dramatic peaks.

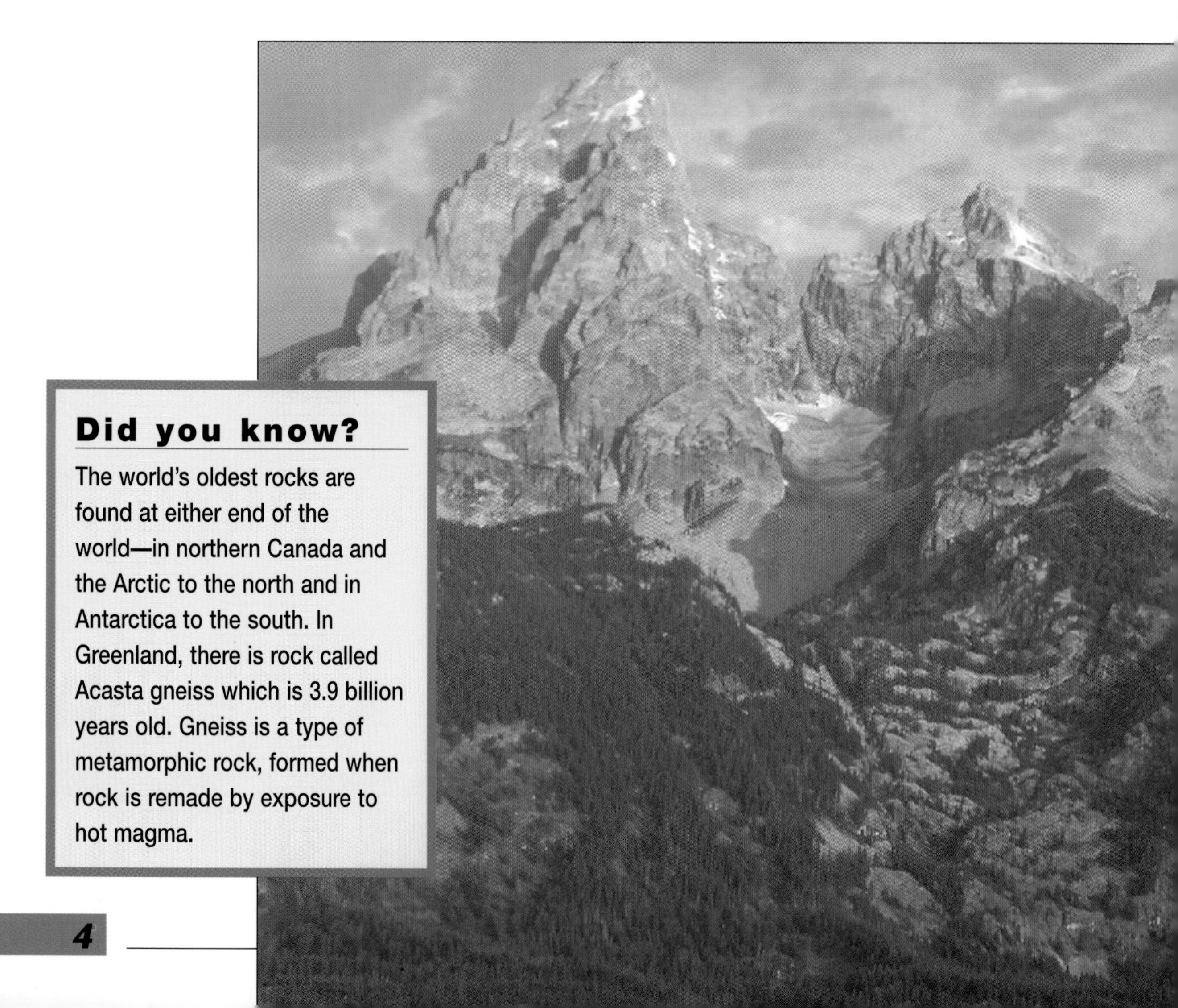

Did you know?

The world's oldest rocks are found at either end of the world—in northern Canada and the Arctic to the north and in Antarctica to the south. In Greenland, there is rock called Acasta gneiss which is 3.9 billion years old. Gneiss is a type of metamorphic rock, formed when rock is remade by exposure to hot magma.

In focus

WHAT THE EARTH IS MADE OF

With Mercury, Venus, and Mars, Earth is one of the four terrestrial planets, which means its surface is made of rock. The hot interior, or mantle, below the crust is rock too. Only its core (center) is made from metal (mostly iron). Rocks contain all the chemical elements, but they are made mostly of silicates and oxides. These are natural compounds made when metals such as aluminum combine with oxygen and silicon.

70 percent of the earth's surface is covered with water, but the earth is made mostly of rock.

Most rocks are very old. The youngest are a few million years old. The oldest formed at least 3.8 billion years ago. Rocks form in one of three ways. Igneous rocks are made from hot magma—molten material from Earth's interior that erupts through volcanoes, or pushes up into the crust, then cools and turns solid. (Magma is called lava when it is above Earth's surface.) Sedimentary rock forms in layers from sediments (rock debris and plant and animal remains) that settle on the seabed. The sediments are squeezed into rock over millions of years. Metamorphic rock is made when rock is crushed by the huge forces that build mountains or seared by the heat of molten magma.

HOT ROCKS

Many rocks are formed as red hot lava spewed from a volcano's mouth cools and solidifies.

Did you know?

Temperatures rise by 63°F (35°C) for every 3,000 ft (1,000 m) further down into the earth's interior. The underside of the earth's crust is over 2,500°F (1,400°C). Even deeper in the earth it gets much hotter. Temperatures in the earth's core are probably well over 12,000°F (7,000°C).

The word *igneous* means fiery and this is just what igneous rocks are when they form. The earth may be cool on the surface, but it gets rapidly hotter below ground. Only a few dozen miles below the surface, temperatures in the mantle—the interior layer beneath Earth's rigid shell or crust—reach a scorching 2,500°F (1,400°C). This is hot enough to partially melt rock and make it flow like very, very thick molasses.

Every now and then, some of the hot mantle rock melts completely and bubbles up toward the surface. Sometimes this molten rock, or magma, breaks right through the surface and spews out through volcanoes as hot lava. The lava then cools and solidifies to form volcanic rock. Because it is pushed out, or extruded, onto the surface, geologists call this extrusive igneous rock.

Sometimes, the magma cools and solidifies before it reaches the surface and forms masses of rock below the ground. Geologists call this intrusive igneous rock because it pushes, or intrudes, into the ground.

Liquid magma forms rock because it is packed with minerals. As it cools, the minerals begin to form crystals. The more it cools, the more crystals appear until all the magma becomes a solid mass of crystalline rock.

Because it is made of tightly packed crystals, igneous rock is very tough and stands up to the weather well. This is why most high mountain ranges are made of igneous rock. Indeed, most of the earth's crust is made from igneous rock. It is buried in many places beneath layers of sediments. But being tough, it often survives long after softer sediments have been worn away. So masses of intrusive igneous rock are often exposed on the surface, forming hills.

In the real world

This is a cross-section of the ground showing some kinds of igneous intrusion.

IGNEOUS INTRUSIONS

Igneous intrusions can well up under the ground forming huge masses of rock called batholiths as they cool. Or they may push their way upward through cracks to form thin sheets of rock called dikes and sills. In fact, intrusions can take on dozens of different forms. Each form has been given a name by geologists, from shallow domes called laccoliths to bowls called lopoliths.

CRYSTAL ROCK

You will need

- ✔ A small saucepan
- ✔ A plastic storage container
- ✔ Food coloring
- ✔ A measuring pitcher
- ✔ A wooden spoon
- ✔ Sugar

1 Measure ½ cup (0.25 l) of water into a pan. Stir in 1 cup (0.5 l) of sugar. Ask an adult to heat the pan until the sugar dissolves.

In the real world

BLACK GLASS

Nearly all igneous rocks are made of crystals, but the crystals are often so small they can only be seen with a microscope. One exception is obsidian, which forms in small pockets when lava cools so quickly crystals have no time to form. The result is a shiny, black, glasslike rock.

Obsidian was prized by Native Americans long ago. They used it to make arrowheads.

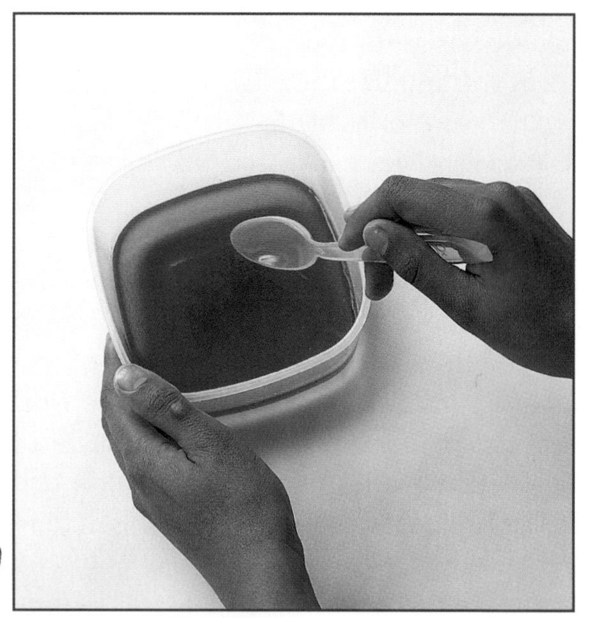

3 Push the crystals on the surface down into the liquid with a spoon. Leave for a week, then drain off any excess liquid.

2 Allow the liquid to cool and stir in drops of food coloring. Pour the liquid into a plastic container and leave for two days.

What is happening?

Rock candy forms in the same way as igneous rocks. When water is hot, it can dissolve a lot of sugar. But as it cools, less sugar can stay dissolved. So some begins to turn solid. As it turns solid the sugar grows into crystals, because one bit of sugar is drawn to another. As the water evaporates over the week, ever more sugar crystallizes. The same happens as molten magma cools to form igneous rock. Here, dissolved minerals rather than sugar slowly crystallize out of the liquid. The more gradual this crystallization is, the bigger the crystals grow. Rocks that cool slowly far underground form the biggest crystals.

When the crystals are dry, turn the container upside down and push the base to break them into chunks. Turn the resulting rock candy out on to a bowl or sheet of wax paper. The crystals you get may be quite small, and people argue about the best way to get big crystals like those in the picture. The key is to leave the liquid to cool undisturbed as long and slowly as possible. You could also try adding a few large grains or chunks of sugar to act as "seeds" around which crystals will grow.

ROCKS FROM DEBRIS

This rock is sandstone, made from billions of grains of sand piled up in an ancient desert. The layers formed as the sand settled are clearly visible.

Most of the earth's crust is made from igneous rocks, but three-quarters of the continents are covered with rocks made from sediments.

Sedimentary rocks are made mostly from fragments of igneous rock broken down by exposure to the weather. Look at a sedimentary rock under a microscope and the same crystals that are in igneous rock are visible. The difference is that they are broken up into tiny fragments, then glued together with a cement.

When igneous and other rocks are broken down by the weather, much of the debris is then washed down by rivers into

Did you know?

Sedimentary rocks get their color from the material that cements them together. New York's famous brownstone and the red monuments of Arizona are sandstone turned brown and pink by rusting iron.

In focus

LAYER UPON LAYER

The most obvious feature of sedimentary rocks is their layers, created as the sediments were deposited layer by layer. These layers are often clearly visible where sedimentary rocks are exposed in cliff-faces. The boundaries between each layer are called bedding planes, often seen as lines in the rock. Bedding planes mark a break in the steady laying down, or bedding, of deposits when the rocks were being formed long ago. Bedding planes were originally flat, but as the rocks are lifted and crumpled by earth movements, they can be bent and folded in all directions. Sedimentary rocks may also have vertical cracks called joints. Sometimes, joints formed as the rocks dried out and shrank. At other times, they formed as rocks were lifted to the surface and relieved of the pressure of overlying sediments.

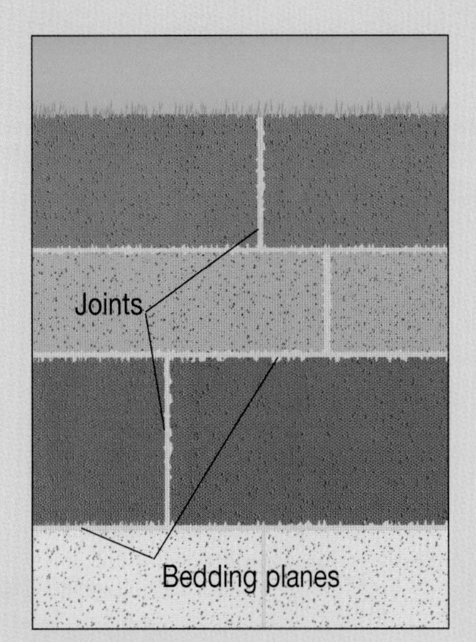

Sedimentary rocks are criss-crossed by cracks called bedding planes and joints.

the sea and slowly settles down on the seabed.

As debris builds up over millions of years, the layers are gradually squeezed together—often into less than a tenth of their original thickness. As the layers are compacted, they begin to turn solid, and the grains are glued together with minerals left behind by the seawater as it is squeezed out.

Eventually, after tens of millions of years, the layers become sedimentary rock. These rocks come to the surface when massive earthquake-like movements of the earth's crust throw them upward to form new hills.

Most sedimentary rocks, including sandstone, are called clastic rocks. Clastic rocks are made from fragments of rock worn away by the weather and washed down into the sea or lakes, or piled up by the wind in deserts of long ago, or worn away by moving ice sheets. Each place forms a different kind of sedimentary rock.

The rock called shale is formed by layer upon layer of very fine mud settling on the sea floor or in shallow lakes. The layers of mud are then squeezed into thin sheets, or laminations, like the pages of an ancient book, which can flake when the rock is exposed.

MAKING YOUR OWN ROCK

You will need

- ✔ Spackle
- ✔ Sand
- ✔ A plastic water bottle
- ✔ A pitcher and several mixing bowls
- ✔ A spoon and scissors
- ✔ Food colorings
- ✔ A shell smeared with petroleum jelly (optional)

1 Mix two heaping spoons of Spackle into about a cupful of sand, then add a little water strongly colored with food color.

In the real world

ANCIENT SEAS AND DESERTS

Sedimentary rocks are built up over a very long time, and conditions when the rocks were laid down may be very different from those today. Continents move slowly over time, and rocks in areas now quite cool may have formed when the region was in the tropics, or even under the sea. Some of Arizona and Utah's famous sandstones formed in the age of the dinosaurs, when the area was a tropical desert, and the stone is ancient sand dunes. Others formed when the area was under the sea or on the coast, and these sandstones are ancient beaches and seabeds.

Rocks formed long ago by layers of sand settling on ancient seabeds are sculpted into curves by the wind.

2 Make two more mixes of sand and Spackle. Add different colored water to each. Place them in the bottle in layers.

What is happening?

Here you are making sandstone much as sandstone is made in nature. Just as the sand forming sandstone builds up on the seabed, you build up the sand layer by layer. Different materials in the environment at the time sandstone formed give it different colors, like your food color. The Spackle cements the grains of sand together, like the cements such as calcite in natural sandstone. The difference is that you do not have millions of years and the pressure of tons of sand above to make your rock really hard.

After a few days, turn the sand out of the bottle. Cut the bottle with scissors if necessary. The sand should now be hard rock in layers just like sandstone. You can make them even more realistic by adding a shell between layers as you fill the bottle. Then when the sand hardens, the shell will be revealed as a fossil, as below.

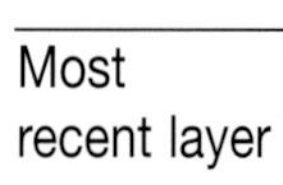

ROCKS FROM SHELLS

Did you know?

Chalk rock is nearly pure white and made almost entirely of the mineral calcite. Some chalk is made completely of microscopic plants called coccoliths, which once lived on the bed of shallow tropical seas.

Near Pammukale in Turkey, hot springs rich in calcium carbonate bubble up from the ground to form fantastic fountains of solid white travertine, as the water evaporates.

In the real world

CEMENT

Cement is sometimes thought of as a modern invention, but the grains in sedimentary rocks are held together by natural cement, which keeps them from crumbling. The Ancient Romans discovered the same principle, adding lime and water to sand so it sets solid in a mix called *pozzuolana*. Later they added volcanic ash to make it rock hard. Most modern cement is based on Portland cement, invented in 1824 by Joseph Aspdin. Portland cement is made from lime and clay, heated together to form cinders then ground to a powder.

Modern buildings rely on cement produced at works like these where lime and clay are heated inside huge white kilns.

Not all sedimentary rocks are clastic—that is, made from fragments of other rocks. These fragments are usually visible as grains or even pebbles. But some sedimentary rocks have a powdery texture and are much paler in color. These powdery rocks are made either from the remains of living things (organic sediments) or from chemicals in water.

All sedimentary rocks contain some fossils—the remains of living things turned to stone—but organic sediments are made almost entirely from or by living things. These rocks are all limestones, because the calcium in shell and bone turns to lime. Some, like chalk and shelly limestone, are made from the broken remains of plants and sea creatures that settled on the seabed. Geologists call these bioclastic rocks. Others, called biogenic rocks, are made by the living things themselves. Reef limestone is coral reef turned to stone. It is built up over the ages by colonies of coral and the creatures that live on them.

Chemical sediments form when water that is rich in minerals evaporates, leaving behind solid deposits. Tufa deposits are left around the rim of cool pools rich in the mineral calcite—rather like the limescale that forms on faucets in hard water areas. Travertine is a rock that builds up as a hard crust around the edge of hot springs.

ROCKS IN LAYERS

Most of the rocks on the surface of continents—at least around the edges—are sedimentary, and each formed at a particular time in the past. By looking at the layers, or strata, of rock, geologists can read the history of the earth in the ground.

The first thing a geologist tries to find out is the age of the rock. Sediments are laid down one on top of the other. So when they formed, the oldest layers were at the bottom and the youngest at the top. But the rock at the bottom will not always be the oldest. Since they were formed, the layers have often been tilted, twisted, turned upside down, or even broken. Different kinds of rock

Dinosaur hunters can estimate the age of bones from the rocks the bones are found in. This psittacosaurus skeleton was found in 107 million year-old rocks in Mongolia.

In the real world

THE AGES OF THE EARTH

If sedimentary rocks stayed undisturbed forever, it would be possible to slice down through them to reveal their whole history, from the youngest at the top to the oldest rock at the bottom. If a column of rock down through the sequence could be extracted from the ground, this geological column would be like a book telling Earth's history over the last 570 million years, when fossils first began to form. Each layer of rock is then a unit of time. Just like days are divided into hours, minutes, and seconds, so geological time has its own units. Eras, like the Mesozoic, lasted hundreds of millions of years.

Cenozoic	1.6 mya Quaternary
	66 mya Tertiary
Mesozoic	135 mya Cretaceous
	205 mya Jurassic
	250 mya Triassic
Paleozoic	290 mya Permian
	320 mya Pennsylvanian
	355 mya Mississippian
	410 mya Devonian
	438 mya Silurian
	510 mya Ordovician
	570 mya (million years ago) Cambrian

were also laid down at the same time in different places. Yet geologists can still work out how old the rock is.

The most important clue lies in the remains of living plants and animals preserved in it as fossils when it formed. Each layer of rock contains a certain range of fossils. This range is called an assemblage. Since living things changed through time, each assemblage can only belong to one time period. So most rocks can be dated from the range of fossils they contain.

Fossils can only show the relative age of rocks. To get an exact date, geologists measure special "radioactive" particles in the rocks that steadily decrease in number over time. The proportion left shows how old the rocks are.

MAKING YOUR OWN FOSSIL CAST

You will need

- ✔ A small mixing bowl
- ✔ Petroleum jelly
- ✔ A paintbrush
- ✔ A round plastic cookie cutter
- ✔ Plaster of Paris
- ✔ A small pitcher
- ✔ A spoon
- ✔ A plastic plate
- ✔ Fossils (bought or found)

1 Clean the fossil, then smear petroleum jelly over the fossil, working it into every crack on the surface.

In focus

Ammonites are the most common fossils.

COMMON FOSSILS

Fossils are usually only of hard body parts such as shell and bone—and are only preserved if buried quickly in mud before they are broken. So most fossils are shellfish that lived on the bed of shallow seas.

3 Press the fossil carefully into the soft plaster in the cookie cutter, so that half of it is immersed.

2 Mix some plaster of Paris with water and spoon it into a cookie cutter to just below the rim.

What is happening?

When a creature such as a shellfish dies and falls to the sea floor, its body quickly rots away leaving only the shell behind. This is soon buried in the mud, which eventually turns to stone. The fossil is rarely the actual shell. Over millions of years, the shell is dissolved away by water trickling through the mud, but it leaves a mold of the shell behind in the mud just as your fossil does in the plaster. Then minerals in the water, such as silica or iron sulfide, fill in the mold in the exact shape of the shell. It is these hardened minerals that make the fossil. Sometimes, there may be no infill, and the fossil is simply the mold.

Leave the plaster to set for a day, then carefully pull out the fossil, taking care not to damage detail in the plaster. You should now have an imprint of the fossil. This fossil, like those above, is the shell of an ammonite, a sea creature related to squids that lived in the age of the dinosaurs over 65 million years ago.

ROCKS IN THE LANDSCAPE

The kind of rock beneath the surface varies tremendously across the landscape. Vast flat areas of northern Canada are underlain by huge slabs of ancient igneous and metamorphic rock. In the Appalachians, layers of sedimentary rock are so contorted and folded that there are bands of many different rocks packed very close together.

Rainwater dissolves tough limestone rock to leave exposed cliffs and gorges.

In the real world

ROCK OUTCROPS

Rocks can be seen at outcrops, where they are exposed on the surface, and in deposits. Outcrops include exposed hilltops, cliffs, quarries, cuttings, and even building sites. Deposits are places where rocks accumulate after they have been broken down into stones, sand, and silt—perhaps after they fall down slopes, or are washed into shoals and beaches by rivers or waves. Placer deposits are durable minerals, like gold and diamonds, that survive in shoals long after the rock in which they were formed has disintegrated.

This is Hummelberg Quarry in Germany, where the fossil of a 100-million-year-old fish with armored scales was found.

Each kind of rock creates different kinds of scenery. In cold regions, tough intrusive igneous rocks like granite are often left standing proud long after softer rocks around are worn away. They then form rounded peaks, high moorlands, and wide plateaus.

The layers in sedimentary rocks also form distinctive landscapes. Where the layers have been slightly folded, they form gently rolling hills. Where the layers have been folded sharply, they form dramatic peaks. Even where the folds are gentle there may be very steep slopes or even cliffs, called escarpments, where the layers have been broken—perhaps by a river cutting through them or even by an earthquake.

Each kind of sediment, too, tends to form its own landscape. Sandstone is permeable, which means that water can seep through it. The rock is rarely worn smooth by water running over the surface. This is why sandstone landscapes tend to be quite jagged.

Limestone landscapes are even more jagged and very distinctive. Although limestone is very tough, it is also dissolved by the slight acidity in rainwater. So as rainwater trickles down through cracks in limestone, it dissolves away the rock to form potholes, huge caverns underground, and even deep gorges. Sometimes, the rock dissolves altogether to leave just steep-sided hills like those in the Guilin hills in China.

ROCK HUNTING

You will need

- ✔ Protective goggles and gloves
- ✔ A hammer and chisel
- ✔ A hard hat
- ✔ A magnifying glass
- ✔ A paintbrush
- ✔ A compass
- ✔ A penknife
- ✔ A notebook and pen
- ✔ Adhesive labels and wrap
- ✔ Rock samples

1 Clean rock samples with a soft brush then warm water. Add a label showing where and when you found the sample.

You can collect rocks by simply picking them up when walking on the beach or in the country. But it helps to have some basic equipment, which you can carry in a backpack. This illustration shows a basic rock-hunting kit. An ordinary hammer and chisel like those shown here will do, but a proper geologist's hammer is a worthwhile purchase.

Hard hat provides vital protection near cliffs and quarries

Strong gloves protect hands

Bubble wrap for protecting samples

Goggles protect your eyes from flying rock chips

2 Examine the sample closely, through a magnifying glass, and note down everything you see.

Safety precautions

Rock hunting can be dangerous if you are careless. NEVER go rock hunting without an adult or adult approval, and always wear a helmet when searching near cliffs or in quarries. Sea cliffs are good places to hunt, but always work at the foot of the cliff. Do not be tempted to clamber up. Also, you should remember when hunting for rock that nearly all land belongs to someone and you may need to get permission when collecting samples. Collecting may be banned in nature reserves. Be considerate when hunting. Don't ruin the site for others, take all the samples, or damage the site when you extract your sample.

KNOW YOUR ROCKS

You will need

- ✔ A selection of rock samples you have found, cleaned, and labeled with the location where you found them
- ✔ A geological map of the area the samples were found is helpful but not essential

Sedimentary rocks

A powdery, pale rock is chemical/biogenic rock such as limestone or chalk. If it has grains, it is a clastic rock; look at the grain size.

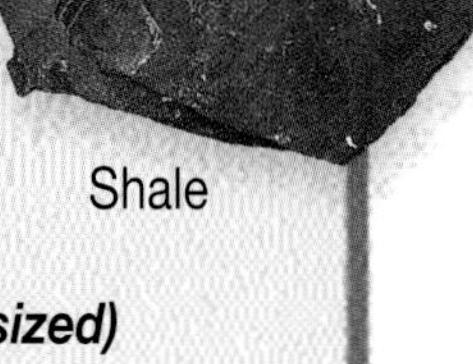

Shale

Fine-grained rocks include silt, shale, mudstone, and clay.

Medium (sand-sized) grains are sandstone, arkose, or graywacke.

Arkose

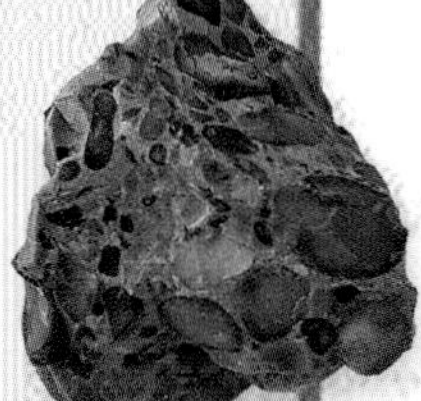

Conglomerate

Large (pebble-sized) grains are conglomerate or breccia.

Metamorphic rocks

Metamorphic rocks are not always easy to identify, because the grains within them have been distorted by heat and pressure. Marble is easy to spot—either shiny white or rippled with colors. So is slate—flat gray and breaking into flat plates and flakes. Other metamorphic rocks like schist and gneiss look banded or layered.

Marble

Hornfels

Rocks altered by direct contact with red-hot magma are called contact metamorphic rocks. They include marble (changed from limestone), hornfels (from shale), and spotted rock (from shale partly altered).

Slate

Gneiss

Schist

Rocks altered by crushing and baking on a large scale, deep under mountains, are called regional metamorphic rocks. They include slate (shale changed by low pressure), schist (medium pressure), and gneiss (high pressure).

Looking for clues

The first step to identifying a rock sample is to look on a geological map at the general rock type for the site where you found it. Then work out whether the sample is sedimentary, igneous, or metamorphic. Sedimentary rocks are made of similar-looking grains held together by cement and are often crumbly. Igneous rocks are mottled with tiny, often shiny, crystals. Metamorphic rocks look a little like igneous rock, but tend to be smooth and dark or light, or may have wavy bands.

Geologists can often identify rocks in the field just from where they are found and the way they look.

Rhyolite

Andesite

Basalt

Igneous rocks are the hardest of all to distinguish, since they are all made from tiny crystals. The character of an igneous rock depends first on how acid (rich in silica) or basic it is—the more acid it is, the lighter in color it is. It also depends on how far below the ground it formed—the further down it was, the slower it cooled and the bigger its grains.

Porphyry

Dolerite

Granite

Syenite

Diorite

Gabbro

WHAT ARE MINERALS?

Rocks are all made from grains or crystals. All these grains are minerals, tightly packed together. A mineral is essentially a chemical that occurs naturally in the ground, usually in the form of crystals. A few rocks are made entirely from a single mineral. Chalk, for example, is a nearly pure form of a mineral called calcite. But most rocks are made from

This microscope picture of 1.6 billion year-old granite shows the mineral grains clearly—black mica, white quartz, and pink feldspar.

Did you know?

Molten magma that wells up from the earth's interior is made mostly of silicon and oxygen. This is why silicates are the most common minerals. Silicate minerals like quartz and feldspar form as the magma cools down and solidifies.

In focus

MINERAL GROUPS

The most common group of minerals are the silicates. They are combinations of silicon and oxygen, often with a metal. There are more silicates than all the other minerals put together. A few silicates like quartz and feldspars are so abundant they make up most igneous rocks. Other common groups of minerals include the oxides (a metal with oxygen) such as hematite iron ore and sulfides (sulfur usually with a metal).

Galena, the main source of lead in the ground, is mostly iron sulfide (iron with sulfur) and belongs to the sulfide group of minerals.

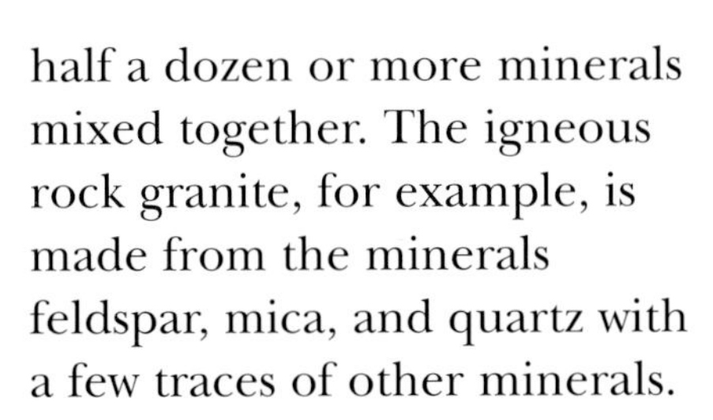

half a dozen or more minerals mixed together. The igneous rock granite, for example, is made from the minerals feldspar, mica, and quartz with a few traces of other minerals.

Most minerals are compounds of two or more chemical elements joined together. The mineral calcite is a calcium carbonate, a compound of calcium, carbon, and oxygen. A few are native elements. These are made from a single element, like gold and copper.

There are well over 2,000 minerals, each made from a particular combination of chemicals. Only 30 or so are common in bulk. Most are present in rocks only as traces. Even so, they can be quite easy to spot because they are often concentrated in certain places by geological processes.

Minerals are much harder to identify than rocks. Mineral grains are generally very small and can often only be seen clearly under a microscope. Also, they are usually mixed together with other minerals inside solid rock.

So scientists must often go through a series of tests to identify minerals. They look for factors such as the mineral's hardness, the shape of its crystals, its color, its luster or the way it reflects light, if it is transparent or not, and its fracture or the way it breaks.

MINERAL TESTS

You will need

When you are out in the country you may pick up some mineral samples and wish to identify them. This is one of the tests you can use. Check your results in a mineral guidebook.

- ✔ Mineral samples
- ✔ Coins
- ✔ Talcum powder
- ✔ Rasp, or coarse file
- ✔ Knife sharpening block
- ✔ Sandpaper
- ✔ Penknife
- ✔ Nails
- ✔ Glass
- ✔ Diamond

1 To find the hardness of a mineral, scratch it with the testers below, starting with a fingernail, to see which leave a scratch.

What is happening?

The scale for mineral hardness was devised by German mineralogist Friedrich Mohs in 1812. He selected ten standard minerals and arranged them on a scale of 1 to 10, with each one slightly harder than the next. The softest mineral on the scale (1) is talc, from which talcum powder is made. Top of the scale is diamond (10), the world's hardest mineral. All other minerals could be rated on this scale by working out which they could scratch and which not. A mineral will scratch a softer mineral, but will be scratched by a harder mineral.

Professional geologists use Mohs's standard minerals to test mineral hardness (right), but you can use everyday objects arranged in the order shown below. The idea is to find where on the scale a mineral lies by testing it to see which of the objects it will scratch, and which it can be scratched by.

1. Talcum powder

2. Fingernail

3. Coins

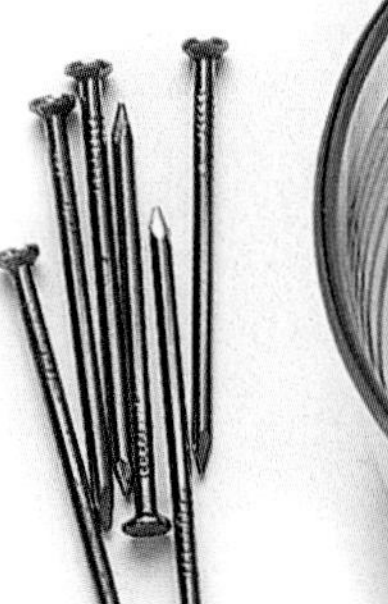

4. Nails

2 If you cannot scratch it with a fingernail, work through the harder testers to find where the sample is on the scale.

Mohs' scale	
1. Talc	6. Feldspar
2. Gypsum	7. Quartz
3. Calcite	8. Topaz
4. Fluorite	9. Corundum
5. Apatite	10. Diamond

In focus

IDENTIFYING MINERALS

Mineral guidebooks often show hundreds of minerals, and pinning down your sample can be tricky. However, there are only a few dozen common minerals, and you can get a headstart by working out where you found it. This list shows what minerals you might expect to find in particular places.

- Igneous intrusions: quartz, feldspar, and mica plus dark colored minerals.
- Cavities in lava flows: quartz, feldspar, and mica plus topaz, beryl, apatite, tourmaline, garnet, sulfides.
- Veins: sulfides, malachite, azurite.
- Old volcanoes: sulfur, sulfates, hematite.
- Hot springs: travertine, gypsum, selenite.
- Volcanic debris: pumice, olivine, augite.
- Limestone quarries: calcite, dolomite, gypsum, fluorite, galena, sphalerite, marcasite, hematite.
- River sands: quartz, gold, cassiterite, magnetite.
- Metamorphic rocks: sulfides, garnet, mica, calcite, quartz, spinel.

Experiments in Science

Science is about knowledge: it is concerned with knowing and trying to understand the world around us. The word comes from the Latin word, *scire*, to know.

In the early 17th century, the great English thinker Francis Bacon suggested that the best way to learn about the world was not simply to think about it, but to go out and look for yourself—to make observations and try things out. Ever since then, scientists have tried to approach their work with a mixture of observation and experiment. Scientists insist that an idea or theory must be tested by observation and experiment before it is widely accepted.

All the experiments in this book have been tried before, and the theories behind them are widely accepted. But that is no reason why you should accept them. Once you have done all the experiments in this book, you will know the ideas are true not because we have told you so, but because you have seen for yourself.

All too often in science there is an external factor interfering with the result which the scientist just has not thought of. Sometimes this can make the experiment seem to work when it has not, as well as making it fail. One scientist conducted lots of demonstrations to show that a clever horse called Hans could count things and tap out the answer with his hoof. The horse was indeed clever, but later it was found that rather than counting, he was getting clues from tiny unconscious movements of the scientist's eyebrows.

This is why it is very important when conducting experiments to be as rigorous as you possibly can. The more casual you are, the more "eyebrow factors" you will let in. There will always be some things that you can not control. But the more precise you are, the less these are likely to affect the outcome.

What went wrong?

However careful you are, your experiments may not work. If so, you should try to find out where you went wrong. Then repeat the experiment until you are absolutely sure you are doing everything right. Scientists learn as much, if not more, from experiments that go wrong as those that succeed. In 1929, Alexander Fleming discovered the first antibiotic drug, penicillin, when he noticed that a bacteria culture he was growing for an experiment had gone moldy—and that the mold seemed to kill the bacteria. A poor scientist would probably have thrown the moldy culture away. A good scientist is one who looks for alternative explanations for unexpected results.

Glossary

Assemblage: Range of fossils in a particular rock.

Bed: A single layer of sedimentary rock.

Bedding plane: The break in the rock layers at the top and bottom of each bed.

Bioclastic: Rocks made from the broken remains of plants and sea creatures.

Biogenic: Rock made by living creatures such as corals.

Clastic: Sedimentary rocks made from the broken remains of other rocks.

Crust: The earth's hard, outer shell of rock.

Dike: A thin, steeply sloping, sheet-like intrusion of volcanic rock. It is made as magma pushes up so hard against existing rock layers that it cracks right through.

Igneous rocks: Rocks made as red-hot magma from the earth's interior cools and solidifies at the surface. They can be either volcanic or plutonic.

Intrusion: A place where magma wells up into the ground but does not break the surface as in a volcano.

Joint: A slanting or upright crack in sedimentary rock, typically created as the rock dried out.

Lava: The hot molten rock or magma that gushes out from volcanoes.

Magma: The hot molten rock that wells up beneath Earth's crust from the interior. Magma is called lava when it emerges on the earth's surface.

Mantle: The hot interior of the earth beneath the crust. The mantle's top layer flows very slowly and occasionally melts to create floods of magma underground.

Metamorphic: Rock created by the alteration of other rocks under extreme heat or pressure.

Mineral: Naturally occurring solid chemical. Rocks are made from various combinations of minerals.

Permeable: Rock such as limestone that lets water seep through easily. Impermeable rock such as clay does not allow water to seep through.

Porous: Rock that can soak up a great deal of water into small pores or spaces within the rock.

Plutonic: Igneous rocks that cool and solidify underground in intrusions.

Sedimentary: Rock created by layers of deposits or sediments, compressed and hardened over many millions of years.

Sill: A thin, gently sloping or level sheet-like intrusion of volcanic rock. It is made by magma oozing between existing rock layers.

Strata: The layers in sedimentary rock.

Volcanic: Igneous rocks formed as the lava from volcanoes cools and solidifies on the surface.

Index

A, B

C, D

F, G

I, J

L

M

O, P

S

U, V